TERRORIST ATTACKS

THE OKLAHOMA CITY BOMBING

Geraldine Giordano

The Rosen Publishing Group, Inc.
New York

Published in 2003 by The Rosen Publishing Group, Inc.
29 East 21st Street, New York, NY 10010

Copyright © 2003 by The Rosen Publishing Group, Inc.

First Edition

Library of Congress Cataloging-in-Publication Data

Giordano, Geraldine.
The Oklahoma City bombing / by Geraldine Giordano. -- 1st ed.
   p. cm. -- (Terrorist attacks)
Includes bibliographical references and index.
ISBN 0-8239-3655-4 (lib. bdg.)
1. Oklahoma City Federal Building Bombing, Oklahoma City, Okla.,
1995--Juvenile literature. 2. Terrorism--Oklahoma--Oklahoma
City--Juvenile literature. 3. Bombing investigation--Oklahoma--
Oklahoma City--Juvenile literature. [1. McVeigh, Timothy.
2. Oklahoma City Federal Building Bombing, Oklahoma City, Okla., 1995.]
I. Title. II. Series.
HV6432 .G56 2003
364.16'4--dc21

                                                                    2001007029

Manufactured in the United States of America

CONTENTS

The bombing of the Alfred P. Murrah Federal Building in Oklahoma City, Oklahoma, killed 168 people, including many children.

INTRODUCTION

On a warm, sunny morning in Oklahoma City, Oklahoma, on April 19, 1995, many of the city's residents arose to start their day. Those who worked in the Alfred P. Murrah Federal Building had no idea what they would experience later that morning. Some had already arrived and were settling into their offices. Others were dropping off their children at the building's day-care facility. Still others were running late, searching for parking spots or running morning errands. They didn't know it, but they were the lucky ones.

At 9:02 AM, a truck bomb exploded in front of the Alfred P. Murrah Building, blowing off the front side of the nine-story building. The force of the explosion caused the floors to collapse, trapping the people inside.

It was a day no one would soon forget.

Timothy McVeigh is escorted by state and federal law enforcement officials just after being identified as a suspect in the bombing of the Murrah Building.

TIMOTHY McVEIGH

Timothy James McVeigh was born on April 23, 1968, in Pendleton, New York, the second of Mildred and William McVeigh's three children. When Timothy was ten years old, his parents divorced. His mother took his younger sister, Jennifer, and left the quiet farmlands of Pendleton. Timothy and his older sister, Patty, stayed with their father. Because William McVeigh worked long hours, Timothy was often left in Patty's care.

As a preteen, Timothy became fascinated with guns and started a collection. His first gun was a .22-caliber rifle, a gift from his father. This was one of

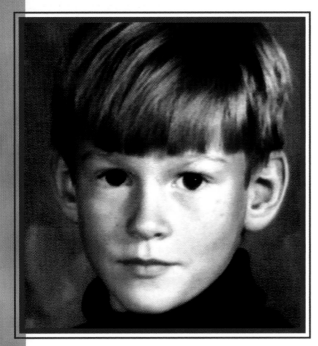

Timothy McVeigh as a child

many firearms that he would acquire throughout the years. A semi-automatic BB gun would soon follow.

When McVeigh was about fourteen, he told his friends that he was a survivalist. A survivalist is one who prepares for an unexpected disaster or attack by stocking up on food, water, and whatever supplies seem necessary. McVeigh collected food, camping equipment, and weapons. Since he had displayed an early fascination with guns, this wasn't considered abnormal by those who knew him. McVeigh proclaimed that this was his way of preparing for war or an attack on the country.

As a high school student, he earned good grades and even won a Regents Scholarship in his senior year. After graduating, McVeigh took some classes at a business school but soon quit, saying that the courses bored him. He got a job as an armored car driver at Burke Armor, Inc. He liked this job because he was given a license to carry a gun. He also took a job selling guns in a sporting goods shop.

In 1988, McVeigh and a friend bought ten acres of land in Buffalo, New York. They told their parents that they wanted to use the land for hunting, but their intentions were very different. They planned to use the land to create a survivalists' bunker. This would be a place where they could store their collected goods.

McVeigh Joins the Army

Around this time, McVeigh became increasingly frustrated. He complained that the American economy wasn't good and that the U.S. government took too much money in taxes out of his paychecks. Without a college education, jobs were difficult to get, and McVeigh believed that the jobs that were available were given only to minorities. McVeigh began to think that he couldn't trust his own government.

He would voice his opinions about the U.S. government to anyone who would listen. Upon hearing his complaints, his father suggested that McVeigh join the U.S. Army. The idea of using guns appealed greatly to the twenty-year-old, so in 1988 he enlisted. Stationed in Fort Benning, Georgia, he befriended two other soldiers, Terry Nichols and Michael Fortier. The three men shared a love of survivalist magazines and guns and a distrust of the U.S. government.

McVeigh *(top row, third from right)* wanted to be a Green Beret but failed the required psychiatric tests.

Throughout his years in the army, McVeigh excelled in both the physical and written exams given to him. His appearance was always perfect, and he was eager to do what he was told. He was the first soldier in his troop to become a sergeant. One major drawback for McVeigh was his prejudice, however. He disliked minorities and was known to make derogatory remarks to them and about them. He habitually assigned minorities in his troop to menial tasks that the other white soldiers did not want to perform.

McVeigh read survivalist magazines and watched movies about overtaking the government. He also bought more guns. Convinced that he had to be ready for an attack, he rented a storage locker and filled it with food, water, and many guns, some possibly stolen from the U.S. Army. It was said that he kept the guns loaded so that he would be "prepared."

The Green Berets

In 1989, McVeigh set his sights on becoming a Green Beret. The Green Berets are part of the U.S. Army Special Forces, which is a prestigious branch of the military. Only the best soldiers become Green Berets. McVeigh trained for many hours. But his tryout was preempted by the Gulf War.

During the war, McVeigh killed two Iraqi soldiers and was considered the best marksman of his platoon. His aim was perfect. It was reported that he took photographs of all the dead Iraqi soldiers he saw. He received many medals for his service, including a Bronze Star for merit and the Combat Infantry Badge for heroism. His fellow soldiers said that he was happiest when he was on the battlefield.

Once the war ended, McVeigh again became frustrated. His paranoia about the American government was growing. He started to fear that the army would discover his storage locker and take his guns away. He became physically tired of training for the Green Berets. After discovering that he had failed the required psychiatric test, he wrote a letter to the army stating that he would no longer try out.

Once McVeigh was discharged, he went to Pendleton to live with his father and work as a security guard. He also sold the ten acres of land that he had purchased before joining the army. Coworkers described him as an emotional roller coaster, ranging from passive to extremely angry. He also continued to verbalize his distaste for the American government.

Oklahoma City bombing conspirator Terry Nichols is escorted by U.S. marshals from the federal courthouse in Wichita, Kansas.

THE THREE SOLDIERS UNITE

McVeigh began sending written complaints about the U.S. government to different newspapers. In these letters, he named high taxes, selfish politicians, and the rise in crime as reasons for what he considered America's decline. Terry Nichols also sent letters to various newspapers and government organizations. He even tried to renounce his United States citizenship. Michael Fortier shared the beliefs of both men, returning from the army with new opinions of the U.S. government.

Major newspapers and organizations receive angry and threatening letters fairly frequently.

Michael Fortier was sentenced to twelve years in prison for his role in the Oklahoma City bombing.

Terry Nichols was convicted of conspiracy and involuntary manslaughter in the bombing and was sentenced to life in prison.

Those places that received the letters from McVeigh and his friends assumed that they were from crazed citizens, people who wouldn't take action and who were "all talk."

Nichols and Fortier

Born on April 1, 1956, in Lapeer, Michigan, Terry Nichols attempted to succeed in many jobs before joining the army. There, he met Timothy McVeigh, who shared his interest in survivalism, weapons, and distrust of the U.S. government. Nichols's stint in the army put a strain on his marriage, and he asked for a hardship leave to care for his son.

After the Gulf War, Timothy McVeigh traveled to Michigan to visit Nichols. McVeigh decided to live there for a while and work in the area. The two men worked at a farm and also sold guns at gun shows held in the area. They both continued to distrust the government and show anger toward it.

Michael Fortier and Timothy McVeigh had been stationed together at Fort Riley. They became friends and shared an interest in survivalism. Timothy McVeigh was the best man at Fortier's wedding.

After serving his time in the army, Fortier returned to civilian life with even stronger feelings against the government. Along with McVeigh, he believed that the government was plotting to create a conspiracy against the people. McVeigh and Fortier's paranoia fueled their idea of retaliating against the government.

The Last Straw

On August 22, 1992, in Ruby Ridge, Idaho, survivalist Randy Weaver courted trouble with the law by attempting to sell illegal sawed-off shotguns. He resisted arrest and barricaded himself in his cabin. While FBI agents kept a close watch on the cabin, Weaver's fourteen-year-old son, thinking his family was under attack, opened fire. The agents were forced to retaliate. Due to this unfortunate misunderstanding, Weaver's son and a federal marshal were killed. The shootout lasted throughout the night. On the following day, Weaver's wife and infant were killed. The wife had been holding their baby when a bullet went through both of them.

Randy Weaver barricaded himself in this rustic cabin throughout his eleven-day standoff with the FBI. Weaver's feud with the federal government was one of the events that inspired McVeigh to bomb the Murrah Building.

Eleven days later, Weaver surrendered himself to the agents. During a court hearing, it was discovered that the agents had acted improperly, and Weaver was acquitted of his crime. Because of the FBI's misjudgment, four people had lost their lives.

The Ruby Ridge incident infuriated McVeigh, Nichols, and Fortier. To them, it confirmed their own beliefs about the government. Soon enough, another alarming event would strengthen the hatred and paranoia shared by the three men.

David Koresh led a religious cult called the Branch Davidians. He located his group in Waco, Texas. Many members of the group were pro-gun activists. The Bureau of Alcohol, Tobacco and Firearms (ATF), a division of the U.S.

After a long standoff, the members of the Branch Davidian religious cult set fire to their compound. They incinerated not only themselves, but twenty-two of their own children. The incident further stoked McVeigh's hatred of the government.

government, demanded that the Branch Davidians surrender their compound, feeling it was dangerous. There were more than eighty members in the group, and they had a lot of weapons. The group denied the ATF's request to surrender and gave the ATF no choice but to take action against them.

For fifty-one days, the Branch Davidians held a stand-off at the compound. On April 19, 1993, ATF agents forced their way in. They were armed and were prepared to use tear gas to force the members out of the compound. The Davidians fought back and injured some of the members of the ATF. When the Davidians feared that they were being overpowered, they set their compound on fire but chose to remain inside. The fire claimed the lives of all the Branch Davidians.

The U.S. government held an investigation to determine if excessive force had been used in the Waco incident. In 2000, a panel decided that the proper procedures had indeed been followed. Unfortunately, Timothy McVeigh decided to strike back before he had all of the facts.

The Waco and Ruby Ridge incidents were turning points for Timothy McVeigh. He felt that the government had used these events to show the American people the kind of power it held over them. McVeigh was strongly opposed to these tactics; he believed that citizens shouldn't fear their own leaders. He decided that he should take revenge against the United States government.

The Alfred P. Murrah Building

The nine-story Alfred P. Murrah Federal Building was built in Oklahoma City, Oklahoma, in 1977. It was named after Alfred P. Murrah, an Oklahoma native who was judge of the U.S. District Court in Oklahoma from 1937 to 1940. He sat on the U.S. Court of Appeals from 1940 to 1970.

The Murrah Building was said to be one of the most energy-efficient structures ever built. It also boasted handicap accessibility, observation decks, and a fountain. Underground tunnels beneath it led to the Oklahoma courthouse and a parking area. Security was very important because this building contained many federal organizations. To prevent potential drive-by shootings, the first floor was windowless. Delivery trucks were able to drive into the

Completed in March 1977, the Alfred P. Murrah Federal Building was designed to be the most energy-efficient federal building in the region.

building to load and unload important items. There was also a security guard on duty at all times.

The Alfred P. Murrah Building housed many federal agencies and businesses. The courthouse was conveniently located next door, so legal business could be conducted easily. The following is a list of some of the organizations contained within the Murrah Building:

- Social Security Administration
- The Secret Service
- Department of Health and Human Services
- The Federal Employees Credit Union
- America's Kids Day-Care Center

Timothy McVeigh targeted the Murrah Building for a number of reasons, all of which made sense to him. The first reason was that he knew the building housed a number of government offices and agencies. He believed that some of the people who were responsible for the Waco incident worked there.

The second reason was the building's structure and shape. For one thing, its facade was made of glass and therefore was extremely vulnerable and easy to damage. The building was also U-shaped. McVeigh assumed that a bomb could easily be placed inside the "U," causing damage to all three sides once it was detonated. This would only add to the devastation.

bye bye buggy

96-CR-68-M
Government Exhibit

1485

This photo of the staff and children of the day-care center in the Murrah Building was taken just one week before the building was bombed. Two of the staffers and fifteen of the children were killed in the bombing.

McVeigh wasn't concerned about the people within the building. In fact, he believed that they should perish. He compared the situation to the movie *Star Wars*. He argued that because the Evil Empire had to be destroyed, the storm troopers were guilty by association. As far as McVeigh was concerned, the Evil Empire was the U.S. government. The storm troopers were the employees inside the Murrah Building.

The Ryder truck packed with explosives is visible outside the Murrah Building in this surveillance camera photo taken just minutes before the bombing.

THE DESTRUCTIVE PLAN

Timothy McVeigh decided it was time to take action against the "evil" government. As far as he was concerned, the Waco incident was the last straw. He knew that Terry Nichols felt the same way, and together they planned on doing something horrible to the government. They wanted their deed to be highly offensive. Blowing up a federal building was the payback they felt was just.

The Initial Planning

In September 1994, McVeigh wrote a letter to his friends Michael and Lori Fortier, telling them that he and Nichols had decided to do something to get back at the government. He

WED 24

asked Michael to join them. McVeigh would later take a trip to Arizona and personally involve the Fortiers.

It has been determined that McVeigh began his bomb research as early as 1993. He read various books on building bombs, retaliating against the government, and revenge on established organizations. One of them was *Homemade C-4*, which lays out in detail instructions for building a bomb. It explains which combinations of chemicals can create an explosion. It also tells readers where they can buy or even steal the materials needed. Another book, *The Turner Diaries*, is a fictional account of racist, anti-Semitic underground radicals who declare war on the United States government and plant a bomb inside a truck to destroy the FBI Building in Washington, D.C. The book glorifies their actions and paints them as heroes. *The Turner Diaries* convinced McVeigh to put his idea into action. In another fantasy novel McVeigh read, *Hunter*, bombers choose as their target a building with a lot of plate glass and an entrance driveway that is big enough to fit a truck. The truck carries a bomb containing a 1,500-pound mixture of ammonium nitrate and fuel oil. The book explains that two cases of Tovex cartridges (the triggers that make bombs explode) are placed in the truck next to the mixture.

McVeigh and Nichols bought a telephone debit card under an alias, Daryl Bridges. They used this card to call different places in order to acquire the materials they needed to make the bomb. Following are some of the calls they made to people and organizations:

- September 24, 1994: McVeigh called Greg Pfaff, a gun-show friend from West Virginia, to see if he could acquire detonation cord. A week later, when McVeigh called back, Pfaff said he had been unable to get it, and McVeigh hung up.
- September 26–28, 1994: Several calls were made on a pay phone near the farm on which Nichols worked. The calls were requests to various chemical companies for purchase of anhydrous hydrazine.
- September 28, 1994: Three calls were made to different Kansas raceways.
- September 29, 1994: Two calls were made from Nichols's home phone to Hutchinson Raceway in Kansas. Nichols asked the raceway's owner, Gary Mussatto, if he could purchase nitromethane. Mussatto replied that he didn't carry that type of fuel, but he recommended a company named VP Racing Fuels, which was going to be represented at a drag race in Topeka, Kansas, that coming weekend.

The Topeka Drag Races

On October 2, 1994, Topeka, Kansas, hosted a drag race. McVeigh asked Glynn Tipton, a salesman at VP Racing Fuels, if he could purchase anhydrous hydrazine and nitromethane. Anhydrous hydrazine is a propellant. Strong versions of the chemical are used by NASA to send the space shuttle into

Investigators believe McVeigh used these fifty-five-gallon barrels in constructing the bomb that destroyed the Murrah Building.

orbit. When hydrazine decomposes at a high temperature, it creates a propulsion fuel, like gasoline in a car. Some over-the-counter versions of this chemical are used by industries to run machinery.

Nitromethane is used in racing fuel. When mixed with other chemicals, and when factors such as heat and concentration are measured, it gives race-car engines power and speed. It should never be mixed with anhydrous hydrazine because an explosion will result. Any professional who handles these chemicals knows that detonation is highly possible.

Tipton told McVeigh that a drum of nitromethane would cost $1,200. McVeigh called Tipton a week later and learned that Tipton couldn't get him anhydrous hydrazine. Tipton also told McVeigh that he had discovered that anhydrous hydrazine was explosive when mixed with nitromethane.

The Ammunition

"Mike Havens" (Timothy McVeigh) and "Terry Havens" (Terry Nichols) purchased two tons of ammonium nitrate from the McPherson branch of the Mid-Kansas Co-op. The first purchase took place on September 30, 1994, and the second was on October 18, 1994. The courts later deemed these purchases unusual because the only other business to purchase that much ammonium nitrate between 1994 and 1995 was the McPherson Country Club. Also, the ammonium nitrate was purchased with cash. In addition, the men did not fill out an agricultural exemption form, which would have allowed them to avoid paying taxes. Most businesses would choose the tax exemption.

On October 2, 1994, McVeigh and Nichols committed a burglary at the Martin Marietta Rock Quarry. This quarry was located on the same highway that the two traveled each day to get to work. McVeigh and Nichols decided the quarry would be the perfect place to steal some of the supplies they would need to build a bomb. They stole seven cases of Tovex explosives, boxes of electric blasting caps, and a box that contained Primadet non-electric blasting caps. These items had been kept in storage trailers. McVeigh and Nichols used a Makita drill to get the lock off of the trailer. It took them a couple of trips to carry the explosives to their truck.

On October 3, Bud Radtke discovered that the robbery had taken place when he noticed that the padlocks were missing from the two trailers. He reported the incident to the police, and Marion County Sheriff Lloyd Edward Davies arrived on the scene to investigate. Two days later, Radtke discovered that the lock on a trailer had been drilled open. This trailer contained the fuel-treated fertilizer that is used as an explosive. Sheriff Davies seized the drilled lock. After the bombing of the Murrah Building, he gave it to the FBI for use in the investigation.

After committing the quarry robbery, McVeigh went to Kingman, Arizona. Before leaving, he rented a locker (Northern Storage Unit E-10 in McPherson, Kansas) under the alias "Shawn Rivers" and stored everything he had stolen. In Arizona, he told Michael Fortier all about the robbery.

McVeigh attended a drag race in Dallas, Texas, on October 21. As he later told the court, he approached a VP Racing Fuels employee named Tim Chambers and asked him if he could purchase three fifty-five-gallon drums of nitromethane so that he and his friends could "race Harleys [motorcycles] in the Oklahoma City area." McVeigh returned an hour later in a pickup truck and bought the fuel for $925.

In November 1994, Terry Nichols robbed a gun dealer in Arkansas who had once been a friend of McVeigh's. Under the alias "Ted Parker," he stored the guns in a rented storage locker in Council Grove, Kansas. McVeigh and Nichols justified this robbery by considering it to be a "fund-raiser" for their plan. They informed the Fortiers of what they had done.

Michael Fortier drove with McVeigh from Arizona to Kansas to pick up the guns. They set out on December 15, 1994. McVeigh told Fortier that he planned to rent a Ryder truck to plant the bomb in. He also said that he would be willing to remain in the truck when the bomb exploded if that meant protecting the bomb from anyone who might spot him. The

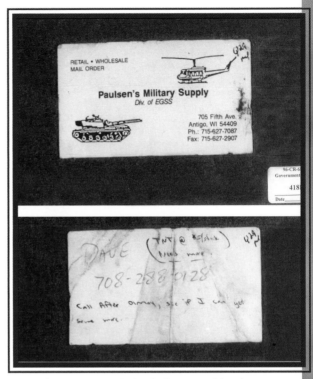

This business card (both front and back are shown) was found in the backseat of a state trooper's patrol car after he arrested McVeigh.

men drove through Oklahoma City so that McVeigh could show Fortier the Murrah Federal Building. He asked Fortier if he thought a Ryder truck could fit in front of the building. Then he showed Fortier where he would park his getaway car—one block away to protect himself from the explosion.

When they arrived in Kansas, McVeigh removed twenty guns from his storage locker and gave them to Fortier. Fortier drove back to Arizona with the guns and the rental car.

The Letters Resume

During this time, McVeigh began writing violent letters, typed on his sister Jennifer's word processor, to the Bureau of Alcohol,

McVeigh's letters to his sister Jennifer were used as evidence in the case against him.

Tobacco and Firearms. He believed that the bureau had played a major part in the Waco massacre. He described them as being a "fascist federal group."

In early 1995, he wrote Jennifer that "something big was going to happen in the month of the bull." In astrology, the zodiac sign Taurus, the bull, begins on April 20. On March 25, 1995, McVeigh wrote his sister another letter asking her to burn the original one. He wrote that he didn't want her to get in trouble for having the one that contained his warning.

Countdown to Destruction

On April 14, 1995, Timothy McVeigh checked into the Dreamland Motel in Junction City, Kansas. He also set about purchasing a getaway car. Complaining that he was having problems with his own car, he traded in his Pontiac station wagon and gave the manager of the car dealership, Tom Manning, an extra $250 for a 1977 Mercury Marquis. The Marquis would be the car he escaped in after the bomb was set to go off.

McVeigh called Elliot's Ryder Truck Agency. Using the alias "Bob Kling," he reserved a twenty-foot truck for a one-way rental to Omaha, Nebraska. In the early morning of April 15, 1995, McVeigh arrived at Elliot's. As Bob Kling, he paid for the Ryder truck and said he would pick it up on Monday. He showed owner Eldon Elliot a false South Dakota driver's license, which Lori Fortier had laminated for him. Later that evening, McVeigh ordered Chinese food from his motel room.

McVeigh is caught on camera at a fast-food restaurant the night before the bombing.

On April 16, 1995, Terry Nichols drove to Oklahoma to help McVeigh park the getaway car near the Murrah Building. Inside the car, McVeigh placed a sign that read "Not abandoned. Please do not tow. Will move by April 23 (needs battery and cable)."

On April 17, 1995, McVeigh picked up the Ryder truck. The workers at Elliot's Ryder had no idea what was to happen. They didn't know that the truck would carry the bomb that would be responsible for the deaths of 168 people. They couldn't know that the man to whom they were renting a truck would commit one of the worst acts America has ever seen.

The force of the blast sheared away the north face of the Murrah Building.
Many people were crushed as the floors collapsed upon one another.

THE BOMBING

On April 19, 1995, at 9:02 AM, the Alfred P. Murrah Federal Building exploded. A bomb went off in front of the north face of the building. The force of the explosion was felt blocks away. People in other buildings were thrown from their chairs as windows shattered from the blast. People who lived as far as thirty miles away felt vibrations from the blast. The explosion of the bomb created a crater twenty feet wide and eight feet deep. The floors of the Murrah Building collapsed on top of one another. The cars in the parking lot were crushed, and some were on fire.

The Rescue Mission

After the initial shock of the blast, many calls were placed to 911. Hospitals all over Oklahoma City called out for emergency medical personnel to report to work. Rescue workers, police, firefighters, and paramedics from all over the state made their way into the city. Many of the finest firefighters had experienced horror in their lives: As professionals, they had been trained for this type of emergency. But at the same time, many had to brace themselves for what they were about to see.

Hundreds of people were trapped inside the building. Some were buried under the building's rubble. To get to them would require great effort. Rescue workers began digging and listening for people who were still conscious. Rescue dogs were put to work sniffing out survivors. They could fit into smaller areas and pick up the scent of a person who may have been trapped but was unconscious and unable to communicate.

Some people managed to stagger out of stairwells. Some fell from the building and were lying injured on the ground nearby. They were in pain and in need of immediate medical attention. Many had shrapnel wounds. Some of the survivors walked away from the building. Some were screaming, some were very injured, and some were silent. Others sat on the sidewalk and awaited their turn for medical attention, too stunned to react.

An American flag
flies amid the
wreckage of the
Murrah Building.

Firefighters
gaze in awe at
the destruction.

Rescue workers
sift through the
remains of the
Murrah Building
a few days after
the bombing.

Fifty people were rescued within the first hour. Around 11 AM, workers thought they spotted another bomb. The search was stalled until a bomb squad was able to determine that the site was safe for further rescue. This frustrated many workers because they felt precious time was being wasted.

A fire department used a hook and ladder truck to rescue people who were in the building and couldn't get out. Federal office managers tried to account for all of their employees. Firefighters knew that some people were not going to be rescued. They feared that the building would soon collapse. Reaching out to hold a hand, or using a listening device to communicate with people who were buried, they tried to give these victims some hope. But they knew their efforts were in vain. Many people died because they were injured and trapped, with no way of getting medical attention.

Almost half a day later, only nine more survivors would be rescued. The final death toll rang at 168: 149 adults and 19 children.

Because the day-care center was located on the second floor of the building, children were the first to be found. It is believed that the children had been eating their breakfast when the explosion occurred. Rescue workers found broken toys among the concrete. The horror of seeing children become victims was too much for many to bear.

Oklahoma's citizens were quick to help. Many were at the scene searching for victims. Hundreds stood in line for six hours to donate blood for the injured at the main blood bank. Food, money, and clothing were collected for the victims and their families. A community came together and worked together to help in any way that they could.

The Medical Examiners

Medical examiners were brought in to begin the identification process on the victims who did not survive the blast. The nearby First Christian Church set up a family assistance center. Family members brought photos of their missing loved ones. They tried to help the rescue teams and medical examiners by describing things like tattoos, scars, birthmarks, and jewelry. Some described the clothing they had seen their loved ones wearing that morning.

Many family members stayed at the family assistance center all night, awaiting news and praying that someone would tell them that their loved ones were still alive. As they waited, they watched the news on television, hoping for new information. Medical examiners had to use different techniques in order to identify the victims in this crime. Because many were buried in the debris, it would not be an easy task. The bodies would not be easily identifiable. The examiners, knowing that families were waiting to hear of the fate of their loved ones, also had to approach their jobs in a sensitive and accurate way. They knew they could not second-guess who they were identifying.

DNA samples were taken from parents, and the findings were used to identify children who were victims of the blast. Dental records were another means for identification. Fingerprints were used but were not always reliable because of the injuries the victims had sustained.

The President Speaks

That afternoon, President Bill Clinton held a press conference. He assembled various teams to help Oklahoma City. The FBI gathered their top investigators to begin searching for the bomber. The director of the Federal Emergency Management Agency (FEMA), James Lee Witt, flew to Oklahoma to help people deal with the tragedy. Federal buildings in cities across the country had emergency evacuations. Security was increased in Washington, D.C.

People throughout the country began to speculate. Who could have done such a thing to the United States? Many assumed that foreign terrorists must have committed this crime—perhaps terrorists from the Middle East looking for vengeance after the Gulf War. Never did it cross anyone's mind that such a horrific act had been committed by a native son.

The Memorial Service

On April 23, 1995, a memorial service was held at the Oklahoma State Fair Arena. Schools, churches, and local businesses held prayer services. Money, food, and clothing

President Bill Clinton and First Lady Hillary Rodham Clinton grieved for those who died in the bombing at the Time for Healing service in Oklahoma City on Sunday, April 23, 1995. "In the face of death, let us honor life," the president told mourners.

were donated to the victims and their families. People cried and hugged and grieved for the family members, friends, and neighbors they had lost. The community and the entire nation were crushed and devastated by the loss of 168 lives.

President Clinton, the Reverend Billy Graham, and the Reverend Jesse Jackson all spoke at the memorial service. At the site of the Murrah Building, people left flowers and notes. Some lit candles. Others left teddy bears for the children who had been killed.

McVeigh is escorted by federal marshals to a change-of-venue hearing. His trial was moved to Denver, Colorado, to find an impartial jury.

THE INVESTIGATION, THE CASE, AND THE OUTCOME

CHAPTER 5

O ne hour after the bombing, Timothy McVeigh was pulled over by Oklahoma state trooper Charles Hangar because his Mercury Marquis had no license plate. Hangar searched the car, discovered that McVeigh was carrying a fully loaded gun, and arrested him. McVeigh had been driving on Interstate 35 toward Kansas. According to the exits he was near, police were later able to deduce that if he had left the bombing scene around 9:02 AM, it would have taken him a little over an hour to reach the area in which he was arrested.

McVeigh was held at the Noble County Jail in Perry, Oklahoma, where authorities found a pair of earplugs in his clothes. Two days later, he was transferred to a federal custody facility on federal bombing charges. Thanks to descriptions from various people and film from a surveillance camera, the FBI had released composite sketches of suspects John Doe No. 1 and John Doe No. 2—McVeigh and Nichols—one day after the bombing.

The Evidence

McVeigh's car was brought to an Oklahoma warehouse and searched. A sealed envelope was found inside. It contained incriminating documents, including one entitled "How to Beat the Government's Terrorist Goon Squads," with the words "The war is actually begun!" written on it. A copy of the Declaration of Independence was among the documents. On the back McVeigh had written, "Obey the Constitution of the United States and we won't shoot you." Police also found pages from *The Turner Diaries.*

The FBI tested the clothing that McVeigh had worn the day of the bombing. They discovered incriminating explosive residue in the pockets of his jeans and on his T-shirt and the earplugs.

With the documents, the timing, the earplugs, and the explosive residue, there was enough evidence to indict McVeigh for the bombing of the Murrah Building. Along with Nichols, who had turned himself in, McVeigh was charged with murder and conspiracy in the bombing. Four specific counts led the prosecution to seek the death penalty: first degree murder, conspiring to use a weapon of mass destruction with death resulting, using explosives to destroy a government building with death resulting, and using a weapon of mass destruction with death resulting.

McVeigh pleaded innocent to the charges against him. His attorney and defense team planned

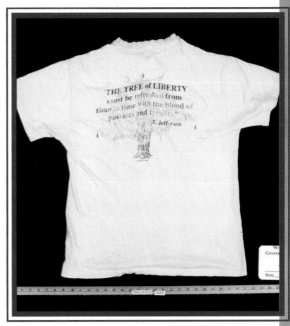

McVeigh was wearing this T-shirt when he was arrested 90 minutes after the bombing. Explosive residue was found on the shirt.

on proving that a third party was involved in the bombing and that McVeigh was nowhere near the crime scene.

The Participants

Joseph Hartzler was assigned as the lead prosecutor in the McVeigh case. He had graduated at the top of his class at American University Law School and worked in the criminal and civil divisions of the U.S. attorney's office in Chicago. Hartzler was eager to take on the Oklahoma City bombing case. He wanted to do whatever he could to help the victims.

Stephen Jones was the attorney appointed to represent Timothy McVeigh. Jones was notorious for his intimidating cross-examination tactics and for taking on controversial

Joseph Hartzler *(top)* was the special prosecutor at the trial; Stephen Jones *(middle)* was McVeigh's attorney; and U.S. District Court judge Richard P. Matsch *(bottom)* was the judge who heard the case.

cases. Jones had defended Oklahoma death row inmates. Now he was going to defend the Oklahoma City bomber. There were mixed reactions from the people of Oklahoma. Jones received both threatening and supportive letters. But Jones felt it was important for everyone to have a fair trial and, as a lawyer, it was his civil duty to defend. Timothy McVeigh would have twenty defense lawyers working with him.

Judge Wayne Alley was originally appointed to the Oklahoma City bombing case on August 10, 1995. By December of that year, he was asked to step down. Since his own courtroom and chambers had suffered damage from the bombing, the federal appeals court felt that doubts could be raised as to whether the judge could be and would be impartial. Because Timothy McVeigh's act of terrorism had been a response to actions of the U.S. government, it was extremely important that he was given a fair trial. If the prosecution could prove to McVeigh that what he had done was wrong, McVeigh would understand that the U.S. government operates in a fair and just manner.

Three days later, on December 3, Judge Richard Matsch became the newly appointed judge. He was not from Oklahoma, and it was determined that he would not allow prejudice to enter his court.

The Trial

The first thing Judge Matsch did was move the trial to Denver, where he thought an impartial jury could be selected. He thought that Oklahoma citizens were too close to the situation to be fair.

Once a jury was established, McVeigh complained that the jury was prejudiced against him. He tried to appeal but Matsch did not allow it. Seventy percent of the questioned jurors passed the challenge. Twenty-nine potential jurors were denied because they were against capital punishment.

Matsch made sure that McVeigh found the jury panel acceptable. He explained that the media can report false information, that rumors were easily circulated, and that it was human nature to establish one's own opinion of an event. In that sense, no one could be truly unbiased. He explained that the group of jurors that was chosen would hear the entire case and make a decision based solely on what they heard.

The prosecution's work was quick. Using audiotape, videotape, and the testimony of police officers and firefighters called to the scene, they easily proved that a bomb had exploded and that deaths had resulted from its blast.

A Third Party?

McVeigh and his defense team thought the best way to approach the trial was to create reasonable doubt within the jury. They wanted to prove that someone else was the bomber. The defense team wanted to call a witness to the stand who would help them show that a third person could have been involved. This witness was Carol Howe. She knew members of a group, including a man named Dennis Mahon, who called themselves the White Aryan Resistance. They were white supremacists who, like McVeigh, didn't trust the government. Howe said that Mahon dealt with explosives and had stated that he would like to cause destruction. She claimed that Mahon told her that he once used ammonium nitrate to blow up a truck in Michigan.

McVeigh thought that Howe could take the attention away from him and make the jury think that Mahon could have committed the crime. In doing so, the jury would not be absolutely certain about McVeigh's guilt. In the United States, in order for a person to be convicted of a crime, the jury has to be 100 percent sure that the accused committed the crime. If even one juror isn't convinced, the case is dismissed by "reasonable doubt."

This did not work for McVeigh and the defense team. Because Howe's information was hearsay and she didn't have any physical proof or evidence that Mahon could have planted the bomb, the court excluded her testimony from the trial.

In another desperate attempt, the defense tried to introduce as evidence the presence of a single human leg found at the crime scene. McVeigh's attorney wanted the jury to believe that the person belonging to the leg could have been responsible for the crime. Once a DNA test was performed, however, the leg was found to belong to an employee in the Murrah Building.

To McVeigh's dismay, there was too much evidence against him to convince jurors of a guilty third party, including the materials found in his car, the residue found on his clothes, and the phone card that was linked to him.

In addition, a marine recruiter testified that he witnessed the Ryder truck parked outside of the Murrah Building before the explosion. After the explosion, investigators had found the front fender and the back bumper of the truck on opposite ends of the building. Both parts were labeled with the same vehicle identification number (VIN). When an object explodes, it is forced to tear apart from its center and fly out in all directions. Because the truck's parts were found at opposite ends, the prosecution was able to prove that the bomb had been inside the truck. The truck's VIN number was used to trace the person who rented the truck and the location from which it was rented. Although McVeigh had used an alias

This is a close-up of the rear axle of the Ryder rental truck used in the bombing. Part of the vehicle identification number assigned to the vehicle survived the explosion. It was used to trace the truck to McVeigh.

when he rented the truck, the workers at Elliot's Ryder were able to identify him in a photograph.

The Death Penalty

The United States court system says that capital punishment is a possible penalty if death results from a crime. It is not necessary for the defendant to have had the intent to kill. Timothy McVeigh argued that, unlike a murderer who shoots his victim point-blank with a gun, he did not kill the people inside the Murrah Building. Rather, the bomb killed them, therefore he shouldn't be charged with the death penalty.

This argument didn't hold water with the judge. The U.S. government states that if a death occurs as a result of an action, the criminal responsible must face severe repercussions. McVeigh intentionally blew up the building and knew that, as a result, people would be killed. The killings were not spontaneous. In plotting the placement of the bomb over the course of several months, he effectively planned the killings.

The Verdict

On June 2, 1997, Timothy McVeigh was convicted on all eleven counts of murder in the Oklahoma City bombing. The counts were as follows:

- Count 1: Conspiracy to use a weapon of mass destruction against persons in the United States and against federal property, resulting in death, grievous bodily injury, and destruction of the building.
- Count 2: Use of a weapon of mass destruction, resulting in death and personal injury.
- Count 3: Destruction by explosive of a federal building, causing death and injury.
- Counts 4–11: First-degree murder of eight federal law enforcement officers.

Two weeks later, on June 13, 1997, Timothy James McVeigh was condemned to die by lethal injection.

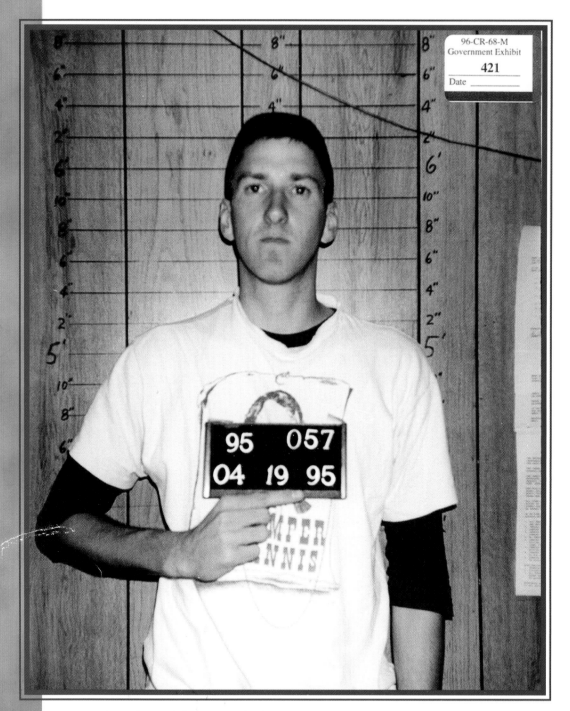

McVeigh strikes a defiant pose for his mug shot just hours after the bombing. He was eventually convicted of the bombing and sentenced to death.

Terry Nichols's Trial and Conviction

On December 24, 1997, Terry Nichols was found guilty on one count of conspiracy and eight counts of involuntary manslaughter. One week later, prosecutors in Nichols's case sought the death penalty. By January 7, 1998, a deadlocked jury spared him. On June 4, 1998, Judge Matsch sentenced Terry Nichols to life in prison. The judge called Nichols "an enemy of the Constitution."

Michael Fortier's Trial and Conviction

Michael Fortier was originally used as the prosecution's witness. He said he would tell the courts everything he knew. In return he would be protected from the death penalty. Fortier claimed that McVeigh and Nichols had asked him to join them. They had described their plan to him as "affirmative action against the government." In an attempt to help his client, Nichols's lawyer tried to discredit Fortier by portraying him as a drug addict and a liar. On May 27, 1998, Fortier was sentenced to twelve years in prison and was fined $200,000 for failing to warn authorities of the bombing.

The memorial for the Oklahoma City bombing includes a reflecting pool *(top)*, a museum *(right)*, and 168 chairs—one for each victim *(left)*.

WHAT NOW?

CHAPTER 6

On May 23, 1995, the remains of the Alfred P. Murrah Building were demolished. A chain-link fence marked the outline of the building that had once stood there. The site received hundreds of visitors, many of whom left behind mementos. Cards, notes, and prayers were attached to the fence. Visitors who had flown to Oklahoma City left their airline ticket stubs. The area became a nation's memorial.

Ron Norick, Oklahoma City's mayor at the time, established a task force to create a permanent memorial. It seemed necessary because of the number of visitors the site was receiving.

The memorial's task force was composed of 350 people. Many were family members of the victims, survivors of the bombing, and volunteers. The task force developed a mission statement for the memorial and gathered input from the community about what the future visitors of the memorial should experience. It was determined that the Oklahoma City National Memorial would be an outdoor memorial on the site where the building once stood, featuring an interactive museum that told the story of what happened that day. It would also be a living memorial to those who survived the incident.

The Memorial

The memorial was designed by the Butzer Design Partnership in Cambridge, Massachusetts. Hans Butzer, Torrey Butzer, and Sven Berg were the initial designers and oversaw the project from beginning to end. This involved trips to Oklahoma to present their designs in various stages to the Oklahoma City National Memorial Foundation. They also created many drawings, models, and material mock-ups of the memorial. Construction of the memorial began in January of 1999 and was completed in June of that year.

The memorial consists of 168 sculpted chairs placed in rows. One hundred forty-nine of the chairs are adult size, and nineteen smaller chairs represent the children who died. A black reflecting pool runs the length of the memorial. At each end stand two bronze walls called the Gates of Time. One is inscribed with "9:01," the minute before the bombing took place. The other reads "9:03," to represent the minute after. On another side is a seventy-year-old elm tree, which survived the blast and is known as the Survivor Tree. Part of the fence that surrounded the original crime scene still stands. Visitors still leave notes, photos, and remembrances as personal tributes.

On April 19, 2000, the Oklahoma City National Memorial was dedicated by President Bill Clinton. Clinton made a touching speech, saying that America will never forget the attack on the nation's heartland. Also in attendance were Attorney General Janet Reno, Oklahoma governor Frank Keating, and Oklahoma senator Don Nickles. Those in attendance wore blue and white ribbons, prayed, and sang hymns.

After the bombing, it was necessary to set up funds for the families of the victims and survivors. This money went toward funeral expenses and travel. FEMA also promised to provide a college education to every child who lost a parent. That means over 175 children will receive a college education.

The Execution

On June 19, 2001, six years after his conviction, at 7:14 AM local time, Timothy James McVeigh was executed by lethal injection at the federal penitentiary in Terre Haute, Indiana. Ten members of victims' families and survivors of the blast watched the execution from one of three rooms beside the death chamber. Some members of the media, McVeigh's lawyers, and McVeigh's autobiographer were also in attendance. Witnesses reported that McVeigh lifted his head as if to make eye contact

This is the execution chamber of the federal penitentiary in Terre Haute, Indiana. McVeigh was strapped into this chair and injected with three lethal drugs that stopped his breathing.

with everyone there. He also stared into the camera that televised his execution live via satellite to a group of people in Oklahoma City.

McVeigh had been detained in a nine-foot by fourteen-foot cell next to the death chamber. During his final weekend, he made a call to his family and wrote many letters. His last meal was two pints of mint chocolate-chip ice cream. He chose not to make a final verbal statement. He also did not apologize for what he had done. Instead, he handwrote a famous poem, "Invictus," which reads, "I am the captain of my soul." Timothy McVeigh was thirty-three years old.

America suffered a huge blow when the Oklahoma City bombing occurred. With enough hatred and violence around the world, people wondered how a person could

"I AM THE CAPTAIN OF MY SOUL"

Timothy McVeigh used a famous poem as his last words. "Invictus" was written by William Ernest Henley and published in 1875. This poem is about having strength in the face of suffering.

Out of the night that covers me,
Black as the Pit from pole to pole,
I thank whatever gods may be
For my unconquerable soul.

In the fell clutch of circumstance
I have not winced nor cried aloud.
Under the bludgeonings of chance
My head is bloody, but unbowed.

Beyond this place of wrath and tears
Looms but the Horror of the shade,
And yet the menace of the years
Finds, and shall find, me unafraid.

It matters not how strait the gate,
How charged with punishments the scroll,
I am the master of my fate:
I am the captain of my soul.

commit such a horrible and vicious crime right in his own country. Many people simply asked "Why?" as they watched the footage on television. When McVeigh was put to death six years later, they asked it again. It's a question to which we may never know the answer.

GLOSSARY

appeal To request a court to refer a case to a higher court; usually done when a desired verdict is not reached.

ATF The division of federal law enforcement responsible for creating laws that deal with regulating alcohol, tobacco, and firearms and arson.

detain To hold a person in custody.

economy A community's system of wealth and management of resources.

enlist To sign up in the armed forces.

jury A group of people who give a verdict or decision in a courtroom.

memorial An object or place established in memory of a person or event.

shrapnel Fragments of an exploded shell or bomb.

survivalism Preparing for an unexpected disaster or attack by stocking up on food, water, and supplies.

terrorism Organized violence against a government or group.

verdict The decision of a judge or jury.

FOR MORE INFORMATION

The Oklahoma City National Memorial
620 North Harvey
Oklahoma City, OK 73101
(405) 235-3313
Web site: http://www.oklahomacitynationalmemorial.org

The Oklahoma City National Memorial Institute for the
    Prevention of Terrorism
P.O. Box 889
Oklahoma City, OK 73101
(405) 232-5121
Web site: http://www.mipt.org

Due to the changing nature of Internet links, the Rosen
Publishing Group, Inc., has developed an online list of
Web sites related to the subject of this book. This site is
updated regularly. Please use this link to access the list:

http://www.rosenlinks.com/tat/okci/

FOR FURTHER READING

Andryszewski, Tricia. *The Militia Movement in America: Before and After Oklahoma City.* Brookfield, CT: The Millbrook Press, Inc., 1997.

Hamilton, John. *Terror in the Heartland: The Oklahoma City Bombing.* Edina, MN: Abdo & Daughters, 1996.

Ross, Jim, and Paul Myers. *Dear Oklahoma City: Get Well Soon: America's Children Reach Out to the Children of Oklahoma City.* New York: Walker and Company, 1996.

Ross, Jim, and Paul Myers. *We Will Never Forget: Eyewitness Accounts of the Oklahoma City Federal Building Bombing.* Austin, TX: Eakin Press, 1996.

Serrano, Richard A. *One of Ours: Timothy McVeigh and the Oklahoma City Bombing.* New York: W.W. Norton & Company, Inc., 1998.

Sherrow, Victoria. *The Oklahoma City Bombing: Terror in the Heartland.* Springfield, NJ: Enslow Publishing, Inc., 1998.

Stickney, Brandon. *All-American Monster: The Unauthorized Biography of Timothy McVeigh.* Amherst, NY: Prometheus Books, 1996.

Wall, Carolyn D. *Braced Against the Wind.* Tulsa, OK: Council Oak Books/Prairie Win Writers, Inc., 1995.

BIBLIOGRAPHY

ABCNews.com. "The Execution of Timothy McVeigh."
Retrieved August 2001 (http://abcnews.go.com/
sections/us/DailyNews/MCVEIGH_subindex.html).

CNN Interactive. "The Bombing." Retrieved August 2001
(http://www.cnn.com/US/OKC/bombing.html).

Coatney, Mark. Time.com. "McVeigh Is Guilty."
Retrieved September 2001 (http://www.time.com/time/
reports/mcveigh/home.html).

Coatney, Mark. Time.com. "Only the Beginning."
Retrieved September 2001 (http://www.time.com/
time/reports/mcveigh/home.html).

The Oklahoma City Bombing Resource Page.
Retrieved August 2001 (http://www.disaster.net/
historical/ok/index.html).

The Oklahoma City National Memorial. Retrieved July
2001 (http://www.oklahomacitynationalmemorial.org).

Pellegrini, Frank. Time.com. "McVeigh Given Death
Penalty." Retrieved September 2001 (http://www.time.
com/time/reports/mcveigh/home.html).

USAToday.com. "Oklahoma City Bombing."
February 2, 2000. Retrieved August 2001
(http://www.usatoday.com/news/index/fx01.htm).

INDEX

About the Author

Geraldine Giordano was one of many Americans horrified by the Oklahoma City bombing. It was an experience she won't soon forget.

Special Thanks

To Ken Fletcher for his time, patience, insight, and laptop.

Photo Credits

Cover © *The Daily Oklahoman*/AP Wide World Photos; pp. 4, 35 (top) © J. Pat Carter/AP Wide World Photos; pp. 6–7 © John Gaps III/AP Wide World Photos; p. 8 © Reuters, Courtesy of *Inside Edition*/TimePix; pp. 10, 19, 26 © AP Wide World Photos; pp. 12–13 © Steve Rasmussen/AP Wide World Photos; pp. 14 (top), 17 © Reuters NewMedia Inc./AP Wide World Photos; p. 14 (bottom) © Oklahoma County Sheriff Dept./AP Wide World Photos; p. 16 © Gary Stewart/AP Wide World Photos; pp. 21, 22–23, 29, 43, 48, 50 © Justice Department/AP Wide World Photos; pp. 30, 44 (top) © Michael Caulfield/AP Wide World Photos; p. 31 © Reuters/TimePix; pp. 32–33 © KFOR-TV/Cable News Network/AP Wide World Photos; p. 35 (middle) © David J. Phillips/AP Wide World Photos; p. 35 (bottom) © Rick Bowmer/AP Wide World Photos; p. 39 © Wilfredo Lee/AP Wide World Photos; pp. 40–41 © David Longstreath/AP Wide World Photos; pp. 44 (middle), 52–53 (top) © Jerry Laizure/AP Wide World Photos; p. 44 (bottom) © David Zalubowski/AP Wide World Photos; p. 52 (left inset) © Brian Terry/AP Wide World Photos; pp. 52 (right inset), 56 © AFP/Corbis.

Editor

Christine Poolos

Series Design and Layout

Geri Giordano